AWESOME
Electronics Projects
for Kids

AWESOME ELECTRONICS PROJECTS for Kids

20 S T E A M
PROJECTS TO DESIGN AND BUILD

COLBY TOFEL-GREHL, PhD

ROCKRIDGE
PRESS

Series Designer: Katy Brown
Interior and Cover Designer: Diana Haas
Art Producer: Hannah Dickerson
Editor: Eliza Kirby
Production Editor: Sigi Nacson
Production Manager: Holly Haydash

Photography © 2021 Emulsion Studio, cover; all other photography used under license from iStock.com. Illustrations © 2021 Collaborate Agency. Author photo courtesy of Jesse Walker.

ISBN: Print 978-1-64876-025-9 eBook 978-1-64739-582-7
R0

For Phineas, Henry,
Atticus, and Jacob.
You are my greatest joys
every single day.
And for David. Everything I do
begins and ends with you.

CONTENTS

A NOTE FOR PARENTS

Awesome Electronics Projects for Kids allows children ages 5 to 10 to explore electricity and circuits. Part of what makes this topic so much fun is the discovery that everyday objects can be repurposed and assembled into real working gadgets. As a former elementary school teacher, I recall so many times when children beamed with excitement after solving a problem or learning a new skill. Now, as a university professor, I create curricula that capture this thrill while scaffolding student learning. Each project in this book has parts in common with the projects before and after it. This means that children will progress toward greater autonomy as they continue to acquire knowledge.

Not only are these projects educational, but they are also great ways to foster creativity. Children will learn the science behind circuits as they draw, design, color, and play using a variety of supplies. Some of these supplies are household items. Others are more specialized components that can be purchased at any local electronics store or online retailer. They are all low-cost materials, many of which can be reused to do different things. Each project contains easy-to-follow, step-by-step instructions, but children are encouraged to expand and modify their creations as many times as they like; the only limit is their imagination.

Think of this book as a "mini maker lab." A maker lab is a space where people gather to design and build objects using Ⓢ Ⓣ Ⓔ Ⓐ Ⓜ (science, technology, engineering, art, and mathematics). These labs are found all over the country, and now you have one in your own home!

Chapter 1

THE BASICS

Do you want to build cool stuff that flashes, glows, buzzes, spins, and more? Then get ready to discover the world of electronics! You use electronics every day when you switch on a light, open the refrigerator, watch TV, or play a video game. But how do these devices actually work? This book will show you how with hands-on experience. You'll make 20 awesome projects and learn the science behind your creations. The instructions will guide you through each project with clear, simple steps. When you see a word in **bold**, turn to the glossary at the back of the book to learn more about it and boost your electronics know-how. As you make these projects, think about ways to modify or change them to create different things. Once you've completed the book, you can reuse all the parts to make your very own inventions! Before we get to that, though, let's go over the basics.

WHAT IS ELECTRONICS?

Electronics is a part of science that focuses on the ways we use **electricity** to do work for us. Electricity can make so many things happen. It's a huge part of our lives. Electricity powers our cars, our phones, and our computers. If you could see inside these items, you might start to get a sense of how it all works. Lucky for you, this book will give you an up-close look at the guts of electronic gadgets. The word *electronics* also means electronic devices and equipment. The great thing about electronics is that anyone can build them. You don't need to have studied all the science in school to make the projects in this book. But it will help a lot if you know some of the basics of electricity and circuits.

CIRCUITS AND SUCH

Energy is the ability to do work. There are many different types of energy, but in this book we will focus on electric energy, or electricity. Electricity is energy caused by the flow of **electrons**. Electrons are parts of **atoms**, the incredibly small building blocks that make up everything in the universe. An atom is made of protons, neutrons, and electrons. Protons have a positive **charge**. Neutrons are neutral and have no charge. Electrons have a negative charge. When electrons move between atoms, electric energy, or electricity, is created.

An electric **circuit** is a system that allows electricity to travel from a power source to a resistor. It's a lot like the way water moves through a pipe. The **power source** is the holding place for the electrons that will flow in a circuit and create electricity—just like a water tank holds water that will flow through a pipe. A conductor is something that lets electrons move. We generally make circuits using wire or some other material that conducts electricity. Most objects are either conductors or insulators. Conductors, which include some metals, help electricity move efficiently. **Insulators**, which include plastic, prevent or slow the flow of electricity. The **resistor** or **actuator** is the part of the circuit that uses the electricity to do work.

Let's take a look at a circuit in action. When you flip a light switch, you'll see a bulb light up. This is all thanks to a circuit. The electricity travels along a metal wire from the power source to the light bulb. Remember how electricity flows like water through a pipe? The switch acts like a faucet that can turn that flow on and off.

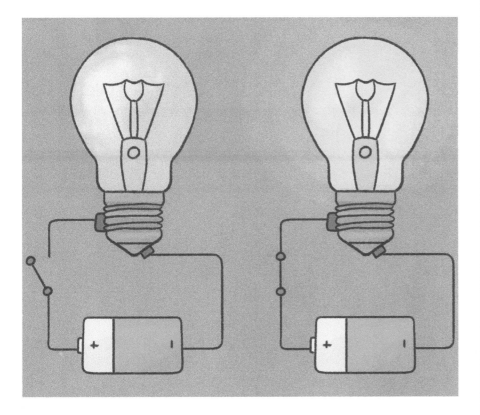

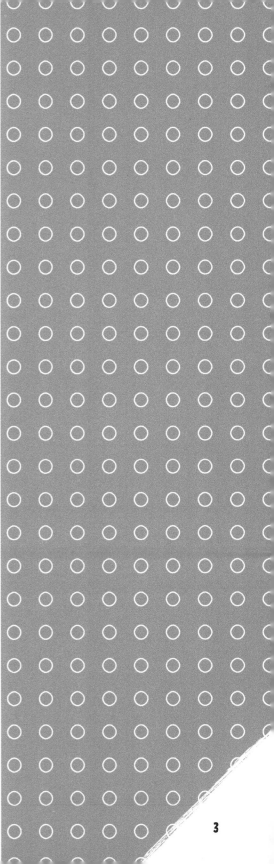

There are two main types of circuits: **series** and **parallel**. In a series circuit, electricity flows from the power source along a single path. There may be one or more **components** along that path, so the electrons flow from one to the next until they return to the power source. In a parallel circuit, electricity moves in the same direction along more than one path. That means it can power more than one component without needing to go through others to get there.

If you still haven't wrapped your head around circuits and how they work, that's okay. You'll get the hang of it soon by building and designing your own circuits!

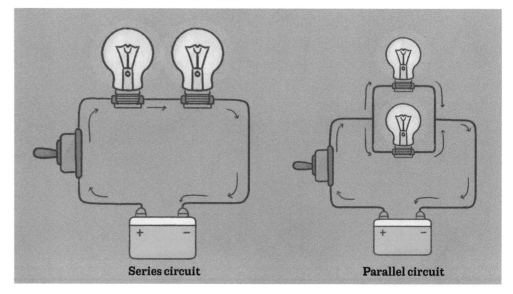

Series circuit   Parallel circuit

WHO DESIGNS ELECTRONICS?

So, who makes circuits and uses electricity? The answer to that question is anyone! Anyone can make a circuit. To do this, you need to ask questions and try out different solutions. That is exactly how engineers do their work. *Engineer* is the word we use to describe someone who designs and plans out ways to solve problems. An engineer who creates circuits and electronics is called an *electrical engineer*. Engineers use a special process to bring their ideas to life:

ASK

The first step is to identify a problem and ask questions about it. Sometimes there are things we can or cannot do to solve a problem. Knowing what those constraints are will help us design a solution.

IMAGINE

Next, we brainstorm possible solutions to the problem. We might make a list of ideas or talk with someone about it. The key thing is to imagine as many solutions as we can.

PLAN

Now it is time to make our plan for solving the problem. To make a good plan, we want to pick the idea we think will work best.

CREATE

Once we have a plan, we need to create a prototype of our solution. *Prototyping* is the process of making something for the first time.

IMPROVE

After we have prototyped our solution, we want to find ways to improve it. The process of improving our design is one of the most important parts of engineering. It is called *iterative design*, because *iterative* means to do something over and over. You might improve your prototype many times to find the best solution for your problem.

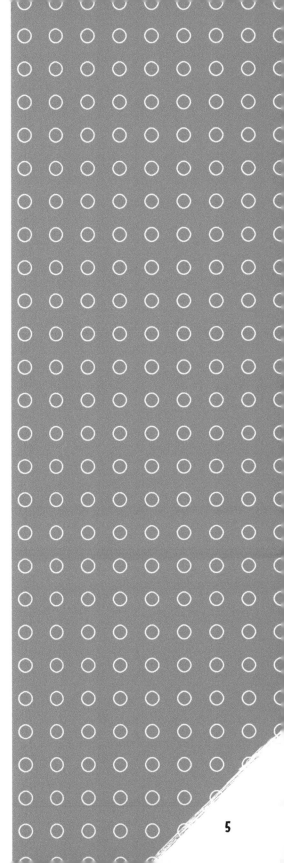

STEAM stands for science, technology, engineering, art, and mathematics. All the different parts of STEAM work together to make our world a better place. For example, the US space agency NASA could not do any of the science needed to safely launch rockets without having the technology and mathematics exactly right. In fact, when an accident occurred during the *Apollo 13* space flight in 1970, a team of NASA engineers and mathematicians worked nonstop with technologists and scientists to bring the astronauts home safely. Just like the NASA team, you will need all the parts of STEAM to make your projects work.

HOW TO USE THIS BOOK

This book is set up to help you learn as you go. This means that as you do the earlier projects, you will learn many of the things you need to know to complete later projects. First, you'll do simple activities and build basic circuits. As you progress through the book, the projects become more complicated. If this is your first time, it's best to work through the book in order. If you've built a circuit before, you can complete the projects in any order or skip the earlier ones. It's okay if you get stuck or find something challenging. If you don't understand how something works, look back at the earlier projects for the information, and check out the glossary if you need more explanation.

GETTING READY

First, make sure you have a place to work. A sturdy, flat surface like a table is ideal. You are going to be working with a lot of small pieces, so having a clear space with your materials organized will really help everything go smoothly. Before you start any project, make sure you read the cautions and pay special attention to them! This information will help you succeed and keep you safe. Some projects require adult help or supervision. Always ask an adult for permission before doing any of the projects. Once you've done all of this, you're ready to start engineering!

DOING THE PROJECTS

You're going to use a **breadboard** to complete most of the projects. A breadboard is a plastic board with a conductor underneath that is used to build circuits quickly. One of the most important things to understand is how to orient your breadboard. You'll see it has letters and numbers that create a grid. There are letters across the top and bottom, and there are numbers down the sides. The directions for these projects are written using this grid. In the picture at left, you can see that hole G7 has a square around it.

When you build circuits on a breadboard, it is important to make sure everything is well connected. If a wire is loose, your components cannot do their jobs and your circuits will not work.

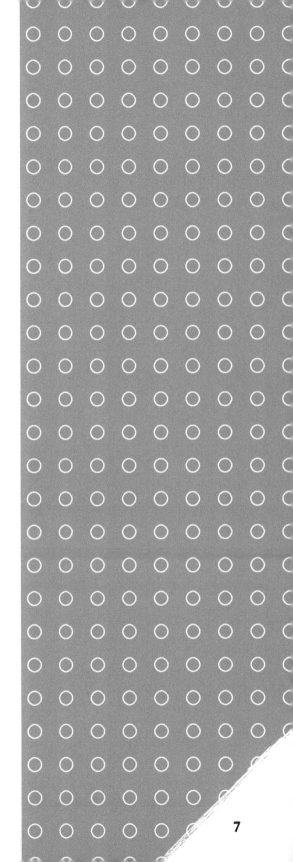

SAFETY

It is always important to be careful with electronics. Electricity can give you a nasty shock if you are not careful. Even though these projects don't use enough electricity to cause any serious harm, it is still important to make sure you follow directions. Always read the packaging and instructions for any materials you use, and keep them for future reference. Never use electronics near water. When using sharp objects or an open flame, *always* get an adult's permission and help.

FINDING PARTS

All the supplies for these projects can be found at major online retailers or local electronics shops. Shop around and look for the best price for the quantity you might need. Additionally, several companies sell electronics kits. If you are using one of these kits, be sure that the components have the same **voltage** and **resistance** as those listed in the projects.

SUPPLIES LIST

Here are all the supplies you need to complete the projects in this book. This list assumes that you will use some of the same materials from one project to the next. If you want to keep your projects intact, you should plan on purchasing extra materials. That way, you won't have to take apart your circuits to reuse items. This list has been organized into categories to help you look for all the different things that are required.

TOOLS & BASICS

- ❑ Scissors
- ❑ Ruler or tape measure
- ❑ Wire cutter or wire-stripping tool (optional)
- ❑ Metal tweezers

ARTS & CRAFTS SUPPLIES

- ❑ 1 sheet of tissue paper
- ❑ 2 sheets of cardstock
- ❑ 5 sheets of printer paper
- ❑ 1 set of colored markers
- ❑ Pencil
- ❑ Sewing needle
- ❑ Embroidery thread
- ❑ Sheets of felt in various colors
- ❑ 2 sew-on metal snaps
- ❑ Clear tape
- ❑ 1 (12-by-12-inch) piece of cardboard

GENERAL SUPPLIES

- ❑ 1 cardboard toilet paper tube
- ❑ White glue
- ❑ 1 balloon
- ❑ 2 large potatoes
- ❑ 2 galvanized steel nails
- ❑ 2 pennies
- ❑ Spoon
- ❑ Mixing bowl
- ❑ Cooking pot
- ❑ Water (1½ cups)
- ❑ Flour (3 cups)
- ❑ Lemon juice (½ cup)
- ❑ Salt (½ cup)
- ❑ Vegetable oil (¼ cup)
- ❑ Sugar (½ cup)
- ❑ Food coloring (various colors)
- ❑ 1 (1-inch) swivel caster wheel
- ❑ 1 (30-foot) roll of copper tape
- ❑ 1 small spool of conductive thread
- ❑ 1 quart-size mason jar
- ❑ 1 bottle of bubble solution
- ❑ 1 bubble wand
- ❑ 1 plastic bag

BATTERIES & BATTERY COMPONENTS

- ❑ 1 (9-volt) battery
- ❑ 1 (9-volt) battery snap connector
- ❑ 1 (9-volt) battery holder with wire leads attached
- ❑ 1 (3-volt) button cell battery
- ❑ 1 sewable button cell battery holder

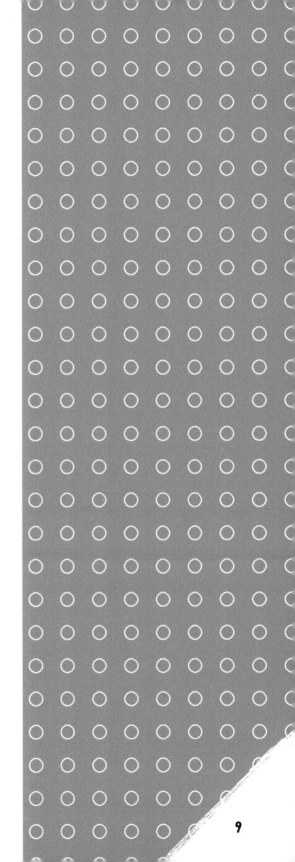

ELECTRICAL COMPONENTS

- ❏ 1 breadboard [we recommend a half-size (400-point) or full-size (830-point) board]
- ❏ 1 adhesive-backed breadboard
- ❏ 1 (220-ohm) resistor
- ❏ 1 (1K-ohm) resistor
- ❏ 1 (4.7K-ohm) resistor
- ❏ 2 (10K-ohm) resistors
- ❏ 1 (330K-ohm) resistor
- ❏ 1 (470K-ohm) resistor
- ❏ 2 BC547 transistors
- ❏ 1 2N2222 transistor
- ❏ 1 (5-millimeter) photore-sistor (we recommend 5K ohm in light and 200K ohm or more in dark)
- ❏ 1 (1-μF) capacitor
- ❏ 1 (10-μF) capacitor
- ❏ 1 (100-μF) capacitor
- ❏ 1 HC-SR501 PIR motion sensor
- ❏ 1 (5-volt) active buzzer
- ❏ 1 NE555 timer chip
- ❏ 2 (4-pin) breadboard push buttons
- ❏ 1 (1K-ohm) thermistor

MOTORS

- ❏ 1 low-voltage, low-current DC motor (with wires attached)
- ❏ 2 TT DC gearbox motors

LIGHTS

- ❏ 5 red LEDs
- ❏ 1 blue LED
- ❏ 1 green LED
- ❏ 3 LEDs (any color)
- ❏ 3 sewable LEDs

WIRES

- ❏ 10 jumper wires
- ❏ 6 wires with alligator clips

TOY PARTS

- ❏ 1 propeller fan (that fits on the low-voltage, low-current DC motor)
- ❏ 2 plastic wheels (that attach to the TT DC gearbox motors)

Chapter 2

THE PROJECTS

Now it's time to make your own awesome electronics! There are a few things you should do before you start each project. First, read the introduction and any cautions. Then gather all the supplies you need and check them off the materials list. Read the instructions so you're ready for each step before you dive in. As you work, feel free to write down any questions you have. Scientists and engineers always keep a journal of their experiments to remember what worked, what didn't, and what their thoughts were. You can do that, too!

Each project has a "Hows and Whys" section, which explains the science behind what you've built. Learning this will come in handy if you need to figure out why something isn't working. There's also a "STEAM Connection" section. We use STEAM to make all kinds of electronics, and you'll find out how the different parts—science, technology, engineering, art, and mathematics—work together and relate to your project. Need more of a challenge? Check out the "Now Try This" section. It offers suggestions for cool modifications and new ideas to take your projects beyond the book.

Are you ready? Let's get started!

ELECTRIC BIRD

Total time: 15 TO 30 MINUTES

MATERIALS

- ➔ 1 set of colored markers
- ➔ 1 cardboard toilet paper tube
- ➔ 1 sheet of tissue paper
- ➔ White glue
- ➔ 1 balloon

Have you ever walked across a thick carpet and then touched a metal doorknob? If you've felt that zap, you already know about electric charge. You're going to use that same charge to make a bird with flapping wings.

THE STEPS

1. Use the markers to decorate the cardboard tube to look like a bird.

2. Use a single layer of tissue paper to cut wings for the bird.

3. Glue the wings to the sides of the tube.

4. Now it's time to charge your balloon. Blow up the balloon and tie it off.

5. Rub the balloon on your hair. This will "charge" your balloon.

6. Now bring the balloon close to your bird's wings. You will see the wings lift. Pull the balloon away and they will

drop. Keep moving the balloon closer to and farther from the wings to make them flap!

The Hows and Whys: Static electricity makes the tissue paper move. This type of electricity is created when objects rub together. Objects can be positively charged, negatively charged, or neutral, which means they have no charge. The electrons in an object are what gives the object its charge. When electrons are given away to something else, the object becomes positively charged. When electrons are taken from something else, it becomes negatively charged. Rubbing the balloon on your head builds up electrons, creating a negative charge. When those extra electrons are close enough to the positive charges in another object, like the tissue paper, they attract. This attraction is what pulls the bird's wings up. When the extra electrons touch another object, they quickly discharge or jump. That's what causes the little shock you feel from touching a doorknob after rubbing your feet on carpet.

CONTINUED

STEAM CONNECTION: You made the wings move toward the balloon. Do you think you could make them move away from the balloon? What would need to be different for that to happen? When scientists observe things, they ask questions like these to think about ways to engineer different solutions. Trying different approaches helps scientists understand more about what they're studying.

Now Try This: Did you know you can charge other things with static electricity? You can even "bend" water the same way you flapped your bird's wings. Instead of a balloon, run a plastic comb through your hair a few times. Then run a very small stream of water from a faucet. Hold the comb near the stream and you will see the water move toward the comb. This is because water is normally neutral, or not charged; the comb picks up electrons when you run it through your hair, and the water tries to "grab" those extra electrons to balance everything.

POTATO BATTERY

Total time: 10 MINUTES

MATERIALS

- 2 large potatoes
- 2 galvanized steel nails
- 2 pennies
- 3 wires with alligator clips
- 1 red LED

A lot of times we think that electricity "lives" in wires. But electric charges can be found everywhere. Even in potatoes. Really! In this project, you are going to make an **LED** light up using a couple of potatoes.

THE STEPS

1. Stick a nail into one end of a potato. We will call this Potato 1.

2. Stick a penny into the other end of Potato 1.

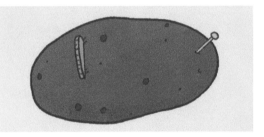

3. Repeat steps 1 and 2 with the second potato. We will call this Potato 2.

4. Clip one end of a wire to the nail in Potato 1 and the other end to the penny in Potato 2.

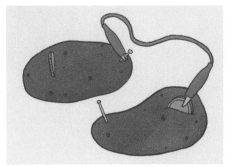

CONTINUED

5. Clip one end of another wire to the penny in Potato 1 and the other end to the positive (+) lead of the LED.

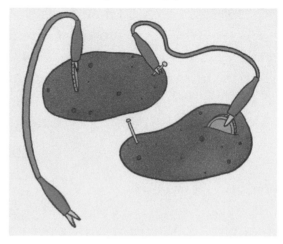

6. Clip one end of the remaining wire to the nail in Potato 2 and the other end to the negative (−) lead of the LED. You should see a faint glow. Dim the lights in your room if you have trouble seeing it.

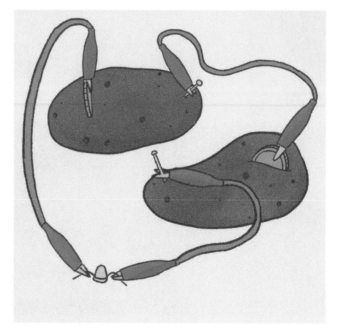

The Hows and Whys: The negative end of a battery is called a **cathode**, and the positive end is called an **anode**. Your potatoes have their own cathodes and anodes: the penny and the nail. So how does electricity flow from the potato battery to your LED? The juice in the potato acts as an **electrolyte**. An electrolyte is a material that allows for the flow of electricity. **Ions** flow from the electrolyte solution, allowing electrons to flow through the metals of the penny and the nail. This makes the LED light up. We use a red LED because it has the lowest **resistance**. Resistance measures how well electricity can flow in a material. Low resistance means an object conducts electricity well.

STEAM CONNECTION: Electrolytes aren't just used in scientific projects. Sports drinks consumed by athletes have a lot of electrolytes. Because electrolytes conduct electricity, they help regulate muscle and nerve function in your body. When you sweat, your body loses electrolytes, so athletes drink liquids with electrolytes to improve their performance.

Now Try This: Try extending the activity to other objects, like different fruits and vegetables. What happens when you use an orange as a battery? What do the objects that work have in common?

DOUGH CIRCUITS

Total time: 15 TO
30 MINUTES

MATERIALS

- Cooking pot
- Spoon
- Mixing bowl

FOR THE CONDUCTIVE DOUGH

- 1 cup water
- 1½ cups flour
- ½ cup salt
- 7 tablespoons lemon juice
- 1 tablespoon vegetable oil
- A few drops of food coloring (any color)

FOR THE INSULATING DOUGH

- 1½ cups flour
- ½ cup sugar
- 3 tablespoons vegetable oil

Wire is not the only thing that conducts electricity in a circuit. In this project, you will explore conductors and insulation with something a lot more squishy. So roll up your sleeves, roll out some dough, and let the electricity roll on!

 Caution: For this project, you need to use a hot stove, so ask an adult to help you.

THE STEPS

1. Before we can build these circuits, we need to make our doughs. For **conductive** dough, combine the water, flour, salt, lemon juice, oil, and food coloring in the pot; use the spoon to mix the ingredients together. Cook over medium heat, stirring, until the dough thickens and forms a ball. Dust a work surface (like the countertop) with flour and turn the dough out onto the surface. Knead the dough until it is smooth, then set it aside.

2. Now make the insulating dough. Combine the flour, sugar, oil, and food coloring in the bowl; use the spoon to mix the ingredients together. Once the ingredients are mixed, slowly stir in the water until your dough is thick enough to make a ball. Turn the dough out onto your flour-dusted surface and knead until it is smooth.

3. Make dough circuits! Make two rolls of the conductive dough, each 1 inch thick and 5 inches long. Then make a roll of insulating dough around the same size as your conductive dough rolls.

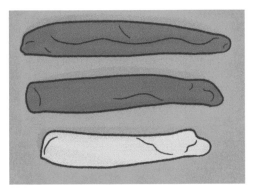

4. Put the positive (+) lead of the LED into one conductive dough roll and the negative (–) lead into the other conductive dough roll. Put the insulating roll of dough between the conductive dough rolls.

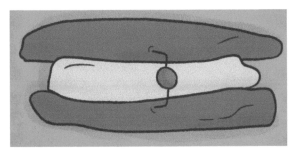

5. To connect your battery, put the positive (+) battery wire into the conductive dough roll that has the positive (+) lead. Put the negative (–) battery wire into the conductive dough roll that has the negative (–) lead.

CONTINUED

- A few drops of food coloring (a different color than what you used for the conductive dough)
- ½ cup water

FOR THE CIRCUIT
- 1 LED (any color)
- 2 wires with alligator clips
- 1 (9-volt) battery

The Hows and Whys: These dough circuits work the same way as a circuit that uses only wire conductors. Remember that when something is conductive, it helps electrons move through a circuit. The salt in your dough is a conductor, which moves the electricity from the battery through the circuit. So why do you need the insulating dough? This dough prevents a short circuit. Electricity is lazy and will always take the shortest path to get where it wants to go. A short circuit is when the electricity takes a path you didn't mean to make and doesn't do the work you want it to do. For example, if you put your LED into only the conductive dough, it will not light up. That is because the electricity would flow everywhere in the dough. Electricity needs to flow in a path to do work. In this case, it needs to go through the LED and back to the battery. That's why we need the insulating dough in the middle. Electricity cannot flow through an insulator, so this dough stops any flow between the two conductive rolls.

STEAM CONNECTION: Dough circuits let you explore conductivity while creating art. You can make all kinds of interesting projects. This dough is much easier to mold than rigid wire, so you can make different shapes for your circuits.

Now Try This: What other components might you use with dough circuits? Perhaps a solar panel to power the circuit, or a buzzer to make a dough alarm. Can you think of ways to combine dough circuits with other projects in this book?

LIGHT-UP BIRTHDAY CARD

Total time: 15 TO 30 MINUTES

MATERIALS

- About 3 feet of copper tape
- Scissors
- 2 sheets of printer paper
- Pencil
- 1 LED (any color)
- Clear tape
- 1 set of colored markers
- 1 (3-volt) button cell battery

You've been building circuits for yourself. Now you're going to make a circuit for someone else! This project lets you draw and build a simple circuit that lights up a birthday card. If you prefer, you can make a card to celebrate any special day—or for no reason at all!

 Caution: The copper tape has sharp edges that can cut you, so be careful when working with it.

THE STEPS

1. Roll out the copper tape. Cut the tape off the roll.

2. Fold one sheet of paper in half to make a card.

3. Decide what you want the front of your card to look like. Do a quick sketch on the other piece of paper. Put an X on the spot where you want your picture to light up.

CONTINUED

4. Now you need to draw the circuit on the inside of your card. Use the pencil to draw the path for your circuit. You can copy the template below if this is your first time drawing a circuit. The copper tape needs to make a path around the inside of the card that connects each side of the battery with each side of the LED.

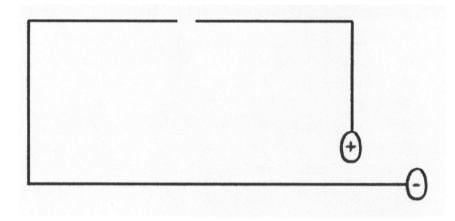

5. Use the clear tape to fasten the copper tape along the path you have drawn. Use your fingers to tear the tape off the roll.

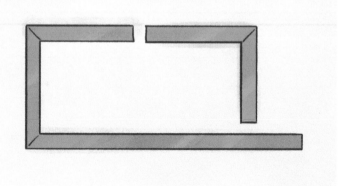

6. The gap in the copper tape is where you will put your LED. The LED has two legs: one is longer and one is shorter. The longer leg goes on the left. Use clear tape to attach each leg of the LED to the copper tape.

7. Now place your battery on the positive (+) circle. Make sure the positive (+) side of the battery faces down on the copper.

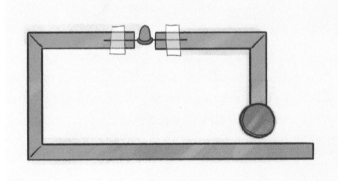

CONTINUED

8. To make the LED light up, the battery needs to touch the negative (–) end of the copper tape. You can do this by folding the paper over the top of the battery. If you'd like to secure the battery to the card, attach a binder clip over the paper fold.

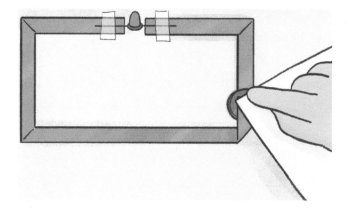

9. Fold down the cover of your card. Gently push and twist the LED through the paper. Now you can decorate the card with markers. Refer to your sketch and draw as much as you like!

The Hows and Whys: The power source in this project is the battery. When we create a circuit, we are making a path that directs electricity from one side of the battery to the other. The electrons stored in the battery flow through the copper tape. Metals like copper do a really good job of conducting, or helping to move electrons along. The electrons travel through the metal wires in the LED and continue on their path to the other side of the battery. When this happens, your LED lights up.

STEAM CONNECTION: This greeting card combines art and science. You get to decide how your circuit is designed based on how you want it to look artistically.

Now Try This: Paper circuits are not limited to greeting cards. You can make a light-up cootie catcher, a light-up bookmark, and so many other paper crafts. Find more ideas for paper circuits in the resources section on page 107.

HOLIDAY LIGHTS

Total time: 30 MINUTES

MATERIALS

- Pencil
- 2 sheets of printer paper
- Copper tape
- Scissors
- 5 red LEDs
- Clear tape
- 3 (3-volt) button cell batteries

During the holidays, we string up lights and decorations. It fills the season with joy and cheer! But did you know how much engineering goes into this? Holiday lights are made in a few different ways. Find out how by making your own light show.

Caution: Whenever you finish electronics projects, make sure you don't leave components connected to their power source. If you do, they will drain the battery and your project won't work.

THE STEPS

1. Using your pencil, copy the parallel circuit below onto a sheet of paper. You can trace the template or draw it as best as you can.

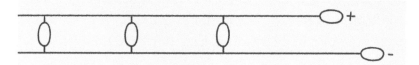

2. Copy the series circuit below onto the other sheet of paper.

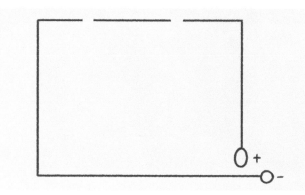

3. Now make your parallel circuit. Apply copper tape along the positive (+) line. Use scissors to snip the tape off the roll. Repeat this process to apply copper tape along the negative (−) line.

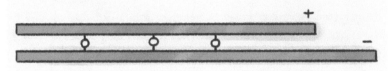

4. Place an LED on each circle between the lines of copper tape. The short leg of each LED should cross the negative (−) line. Attach the short legs to the wire with clear tape. Then use clear tape to attach the long legs to the positive (+) line.

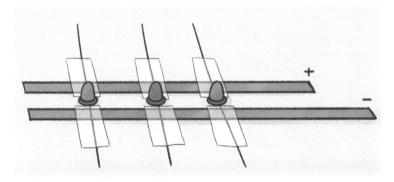

5. Place a battery on the circle at the end of the positive (+) line. The positive (+) side of the battery should be facing down on the copper. Fold the end of the negative (−) line over the battery. The negative (−) line touches

CONTINUED

the negative (−) side of the battery. You've made a parallel circuit!

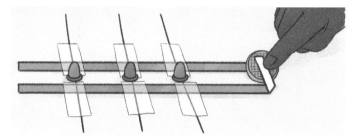

6. Now make your series circuit. Apply the copper tape along the lines. You need to leave gaps for the LEDs. If your copper tape crosses a gap, your circuit won't work.

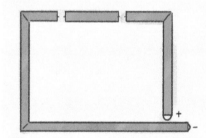

7. Place an LED in each gap. The long leg of each LED goes on the left. This will make your lights go in the same direction.

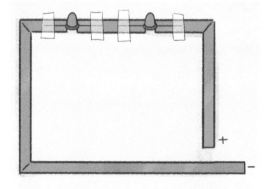

8. Place a battery on the circle at the end of the positive (+) line. The positive (+) side of the battery should face down on the copper tape. Then stack another battery on top of this battery. Make sure the positive (+) side of this battery faces down, too.

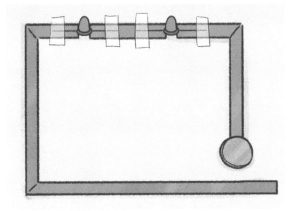

9. Fold the negative (–) line of your circuit over the stack of batteries. This connects the negative (–) line to the negative (–) side of the battery stack. You've made a series circuit!

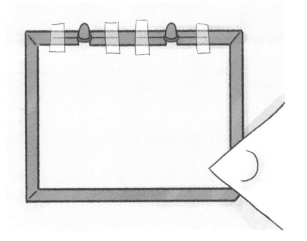

CONTINUED

The Hows and Whys: Did you notice that the parallel circuit uses one battery to light three LEDs, but the series circuit needs two batteries to light fewer LEDs? Why is that? Well, different circuits need different amounts of power. A series circuit forces all the electricity through each component. That means you need more power to move the energy through the first LED to get the second LED to light up. In the parallel circuit, the energy flows along the copper tape, so it takes less power to turn the lightbulbs on. It also means that if one light goes out, the others can still stay lit. This is not the case with the series circuit. If one light in a series circuit goes out, none of them will light up.

STEAM CONNECTION: Holiday lights used to be made in series circuits, which made it very hard for folks when a lightbulb went out. Today, most holiday lights are set up in parallel circuits. If one light goes out, it doesn't ruin the whole display. It's also much easier to replace a light in a parallel circuit. This is a good example of how we use the iterative engineering process to solve everyday problems.

Now Try This: How many LEDs can you light up in parallel versus series circuits? Does the number of LEDs change based on the color of the lights? Try using only red bulbs for one circuit and only blue for the other. The number of bulbs you can light up will change because different colors of light have different levels of resistance.

CIRCUIT BRACELET

Total time: 1 HOUR
45 MINUTES

MATERIALS

- 1 sheet of felt
- Scissors
- Sewing needle
- 1 small spool of conductive thread
- 2 sew-on metal snaps
- 3 sewable LEDs
- 1 sewable button cell battery holder
- Embroidery thread
- 1 (3-volt) button cell battery

By now, you've designed circuits. You've built circuits. But have you ever *worn* a circuit? In this project, you will sew a circuit bracelet that lights up your wrist!

! Caution: When you sew, be careful not to poke yourself with the sharp needle. If you need any help sewing, ask an adult. Sewable circuits are washable, but make sure you take the battery out before washing. Do not put the bracelet in the dryer.

THE STEPS

1. Cut a strip of felt that is long enough to wrap around your wrist and overlap at the ends by 1 to 2 inches.

2. Now you need to sew your circuit. First, follow the template below to lay out the pieces on your work surface. This is how the pieces will be arranged when they are sewn on your strip of felt.

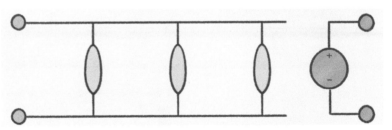

3. Each snap contains two pieces that "snap" together: the piece with the little knob sticking up is called the *ball* and the other piece is called the *socket*. Using your needle

CONTINUED

and conductive thread, sew the socket of your first snap onto your felt strip. (Check out the "How to Sew" section of this project on page 37 if you need help.)

4. Follow the template below to stitch a line of conductive thread to the spot where you will place your first LED. Then sew the negative (–) LED loop onto the felt strip. You need to sew through each LED loop **3 times** before you continue stitching to the next LED.

5. Continue stitching the line to your next LED. Again, sew through the negative (–) loop 3 times to attach the LED.

6. Repeat step 5 to sew the third LED onto the felt strip. Continue the line of conductive thread with a few more stitches. Then tie a knot and cut off the excess thread. You now have the negative (–) line of your circuit!

7. Now you will sew the positive (+) line of your circuit. Repeat step 3 to sew the socket of your second snap onto the felt strip. Then, using the following template as a guide, sew down the positive (+) loops of each LED.

Remember to stitch each loop 3 times. Once you have completed the line, tie a knot and cut off the excess thread.

8. It's time to attach the battery holder. Before you stitch the holder to the felt strip, make sure the positive (+) side lines up with, **but does not touch**, the positive (+) line on your bracelet. There should be a gap between the line and the battery holder, as shown on the template above. Sew down the battery with conductive thread, using 3 stitches for each corner.

9. Follow the template to sew a positive (+) line and a negative (−) line from the battery holder to each of the remaining snaps. Sew the ball of each snap onto the felt strip.

10. Now you can decorate your bracelet! Cut various shapes out of felt, and sew them onto the bracelet in any pattern with embroidery thread.

11. Ready to light up your bracelet? Put your battery in the battery holder with the positive (+) side facing up. Then wrap the bracelet around your wrist and snap the snaps to secure it.

CONTINUED

The Hows and Whys: Parallel circuits have two separate lines: one positive and one negative. The positive line connects the positive loops of the LEDs to the positive side of the battery. The negative line connects the negative loops of the LEDs to the negative side of the battery. When we connect the two sides through our **switch**, the circuit is complete and the LEDs light up. A switch is any break in a circuit that stops and starts the flow of electrons. The snaps in your bracelet are the switch for this circuit. When the bracelet snaps around your wrist, the battery is connected to the LEDs and allows them to light up.

STEAM CONNECTION: Your bracelet is a piece of electronic fashion. Fashion relies on STEAM. Designers use their artistic skills to draw how clothing will look. They use math to figure out the measurements. Big machines using electronics sew fabrics together. This technology makes clothes that people wear every day.

Now Try This: The number of projects you can make with sewable circuits is limitless! You can sew light-up shirts, bags, quilts, and many other things. You can even use a tiny computer called a **microprocessor** to make programmable sewing projects, like a lunch box that senses temperature. Flip to the resources section on page 107 to find out more about these projects.

HOW TO SEW

1. Thread your needle: Insert the end of the thread through the hole in the needle. This hole is called the *eye*.

2. Once the thread is through the eye, tie both ends of the thread together in a knot.

3. To start sewing, gently poke the pointy end of your needle through the underside of the fabric. Pull the needle up through the fabric.

4. Then move your needle forward about ½ inch and bring the pointy end down through the fabric. This will make your first stitch.

5. Keep repeating to make more stitches by bringing the needle up through the underside of the fabric, then back down through the top of the fabric.

BREADBOARD FLASHLIGHT

Total time: 30 MINUTES

MATERIALS

- Breadboard
- 1 LED (any color)
- 1 (1K-ohm) resistor
- 1 (9-volt) battery
- 1 (9-volt) battery snap connector
- 1 jumper wire
- 1 sheet of cardstock
- Clear tape

A breadboard is a base that lets you make all kinds of different circuits. To get the hang of it, let's start with a simple project: building a flashlight with a single LED.

Caution: When working with electrical components, always check the packaging for warnings. Do not connect an LED directly to a 9-volt battery. Always use a resistor, which reduces the flow of the electrical **current**, so you don't get shocked.

THE STEPS

1. Plug the short lead of the LED into E1 and the long lead into F1.

2. Place the resistor between H1 and the negative (−) blue channel on the right-hand side. The resistor helps control the amount of energy that reaches the LED to stop it from bursting.

3. Place the jumper wire between A1 and the positive (+) channel on the left-hand side.

CONTINUED

4. Connect the battery to the battery snap. Plug the red wire into the bottom of the positive (+) channel on the left-hand side.

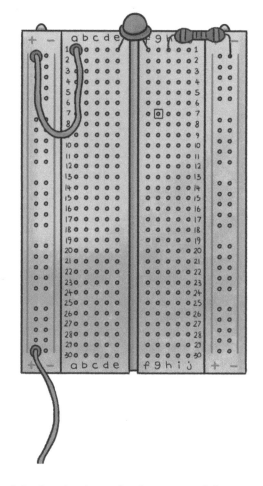

5. Plug the black wire into the bottom of the negative (–) channel on the right-hand side. The LED lights up!

6. Now start to assemble your flashlight. Gently bend the legs of the LED to make the bulb hang over the top of the breadboard.

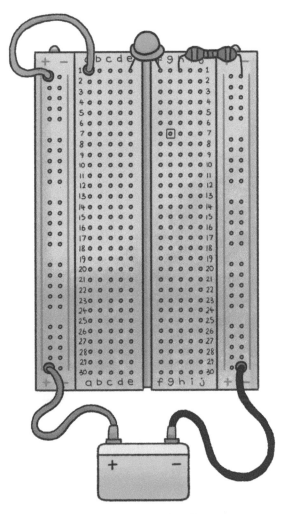

7. Using the cardstock, make a tube that wraps around your breadboard with the LED at the top. Tape the overlapping side of the cardstock to the tube.

CONTINUED

The Hows and Whys: Breadboards have lots of holes that you can plug components and wires into. Underneath the holes, there are lots of copper strips. The copper can conduct the electricity from the power source to your component. Now you can make any number of circuit projects with more ease.

STEAM CONNECTION: The flashlight you made is a quick prototype. Making prototypes of everyday objects helps you understand how they work.

Now Try This: You can make a lot of different lights with a breadboard. Maybe you want to make a small reading lamp. To do that, you should probably tape the connections so everything stays in place. How else could you modify this project?

BEDROOM DOORBELL

Total time: 10 MINUTES

MATERIALS

- Breadboard
- 1 (5-volt) active buzzer
- 1 (4-pin) breadboard push button
- 1 (9-volt) battery
- 1 (9-volt) battery holder with wire leads attached

Need some privacy? You can stop people from barging into your room with a doorbell! When someone pushes the button, the doorbell will buzz to let you know they are at the door. Breadboards let you use many different objects to do work. The objects that do work are called **actuators**. Let's put some to use.

! **Caution:** Always check your batteries to make sure they are the correct voltage. If too much electricity goes through the circuit, it can break any actuators. When working with electrical components, always check the packaging for warnings.

THE STEPS

1. Plug the long lead of the buzzer into J10 and the short lead into H8.

CONTINUED

2. Place your breadboard push button between E6, F6, E8, and F8.

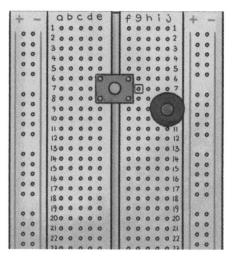

3. Put the battery in the battery holder. Then plug the positive (+) wire from the battery holder into F10 and the negative (−) wire into D6.

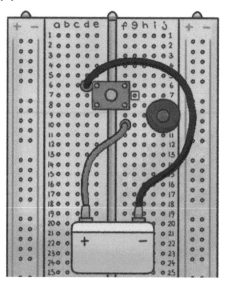

The Hows and Whys: Breadboards have metal plates inside them that allow quick, easy connections between a power source and an actuator. When you connect the negative side of the battery to the negative sides of the buzzer and the button, you can use the button to complete the circuit. When the button is pressed, it connects the positive sides. The circuit is completed.

STEAM CONNECTION: This project is a good example of how we can use sound in our circuits. Once we understand that sound can be a part of electronics, we think about creating circuits that make music.

Now Try This: What other things could you make happen when you push a button? There are so many ways for you to modify this basic design. You could make a doorbell that uses light. This device is often used by people who are deaf or hearing-impaired instead of a ringing doorbell. A flashing light lets them know someone is at the door.

BREADBOARD NIGHTLIGHT

Total time: 30 MINUTES

MATERIALS

- Breadboard
- 1 (470K-ohm) resistor
- 1 blue LED
- 1 BC547 transistor
- 1 (5-millimeter) photoresistor
- 1 (100K-ohm) resistor
- 1 (9-volt) battery
- 1 (9-volt) battery pack with wire leads attached

Make your own glowing nightlight with your breadboard. You can even control its brightness with a dimmer.

Caution: Always check your batteries to make sure they are the correct voltage. If too much electricity goes through the circuit, it can break components. When working with electrical components, always check the packaging for warnings.

THE STEPS

1. Place the 470K-ohm resistor between A5 and A10.

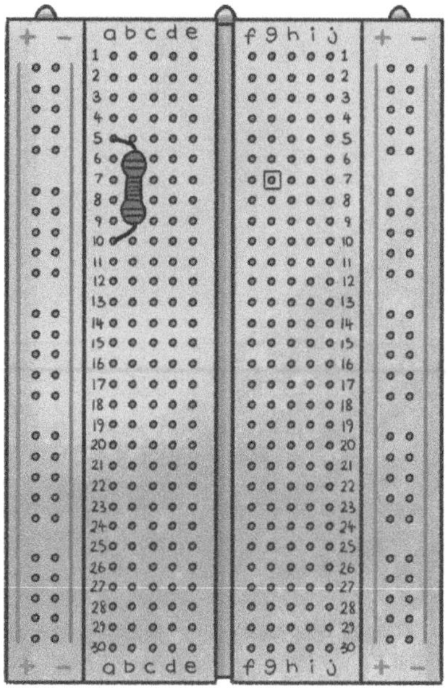

2. Plug the short leg of the LED into B12 and the long leg into B10.

3. Place the **transistor** between C12, C14, and C16. The flat side of the transistor should face away from the LED.

CONTINUED

4. Place the photoresistor between E14 and E16.

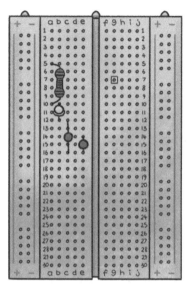

5. Place the 100K-ohm resistor between D5 and D14.

6. Put the battery in the battery holder. Plug the negative (–) wire from the battery holder into E5 and the positive (+) wire into A16. Now turn the lights off in the room and watch your nightlight glow!

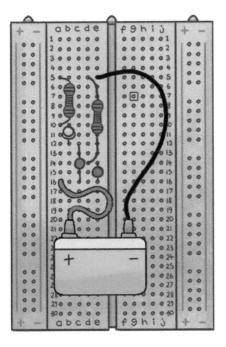

The Hows and Whys: The **photoresistor** measures the light around it. In the dark, its resistance is very high. The resistance drops when it is exposed to light. In this circuit, the photoresistor measures when the room is dark and lights the LED.

CONTINUED

STEAM CONNECTION: Before electricity, people had to hang lamps and lanterns outside their homes when it got dark. Today, thanks to modern engineering and technology, streetlights switch on automatically. Many of these lights have photoresistors like the one you used in this project. When the sun goes down, the streetlights turn on to keep neighborhoods lit through the night.

Now Try This: In this project, the photoresistor senses the lack of light and turns on your LED. There are many ways to use this type of circuit design. What if the LED were replaced with a buzzer? It could buzz to remind you to get ready for bed. How else could it be used in your daily life?

SPY SENSOR

Total time: 30 MINUTES

MATERIALS

- 3 jumper wires
- Ruler
- Wire cutter or wire-stripping tool (optional)
- 1 HC-SR501 PIR motion sensor
- Clear tape
- Breadboard
- 1 (9-volt) battery
- 1 (9-volt) battery pack with wire leads attached
- 1 LED (any color)
- 1 (220-ohm) resistor
- 1 (5-volt) active buzzer

Do you want to keep your stuff safe when you're not around? Use secret spy technology to protect your things! In this project, your breadboard circuit will sound an alarm when someone opens your door or moves an object.

Caution: Always check your batteries to make sure they are the correct voltage. If too much electricity goes through the circuit, it can break components. When working with electrical components, always check the packaging for warnings. You may or may not need to use a wire cutter or wire-stripping tool for this project. It all depends on whether enough wire is exposed for you to work with. If you need more exposed wire, ask an adult to help you use a wire cutter or wire-stripping tool, since these tools can be very sharp.

THE STEPS

1. Check your jumper wires to see if they will work for this project. There should be ½ inch of metal exposed at the ends. If you measure the wire and find that you need to expose more metal, ask an adult to help you peel off the plastic from the outside of the wire using the wire cutter or wire-stripping tool.

2. Make little loops out of the exposed ends of the wire.

CONTINUED

3. Place a loop from each wire over each pin on the motion **sensor**. Make sure each loop is twisted tightly onto each pin. You can apply a piece of tape over the wires to help connect them to the pins.

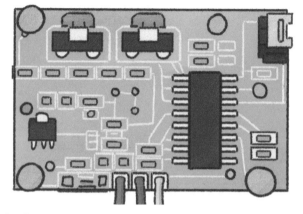

4. Put the battery in the battery holder. Plug the red wire from the battery pack into the bottom of the positive (+) channel on the right-hand side. Plug the black wire into the negative (−) channel on the left-hand side.

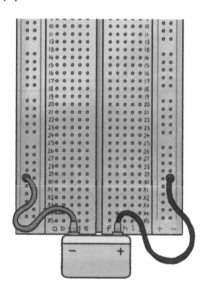

AWESOME ELECTRONICS PROJECTS FOR KIDS

5. Plug the positive (+) lead of the LED into F35 and the negative (−) lead into E35. This bridges the middle of your board.

6. Place the resistor between C35 and the negative (−) channel on the left-hand side. It should be in the same column as the black wire from the battery holder.

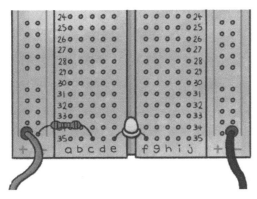

7. Place the motion sensor next to your breadboard, near row 1. Make sure the motion sensor is oriented with the pins at the bottom. Put the leftmost wire into the outside negative (−) line to which your battery is connected in row 35. Put the middle wire into J35. Put the rightmost wire into the right-hand positive (+) channel to which your battery is connected.

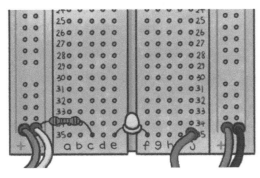

CONTINUED

The Hows and Whys: The motion sensor in this project detects **infrared**. That means it is looking for changes in the light and heat energy around it. When a warm-blooded animal, like a human, comes near it, the motion sensor detects these changes and the alarm sounds. In your circuit, it sends a signal to the breadboard that completes the circuit and lights up the LED.

STEAM CONNECTION: Motion sensors help people monitor many things. Security systems that help keep us safe use motion sensors. You can even see a motion sensor at work when you use a hands-free paper towel dispenser. Using science to solve problems or make our lives easier is an important example of technology.

Now Try This: A motion sensor is handy for different tasks. Maybe you want to see what your pet does when you are not at home. You could use a microprocessor to program a camera to turn on when motion is detected. How would you do this to track your pet?

FIREFLY JAR

Total time: 1 HOUR

MATERIALS

- Breadboard
- 1 NE555 timer chip
- 3 jumper wires
- 1 (1K-ohm) resistor
- 2 (10K-ohm) resistors
- 1 LED (any color)
- 1 (100-µF) capacitor
- 1 (9-volt) battery
- 1 (9-volt) battery holder with wire leads attached
- 1 sheet of printer paper
- 1 set of colored markers
- Scissors
- Clear tape
- 1 quart-size mason jar

In this project, you are going to use a **capacitor** to make an LED blink on and off, all on its own. When you put this electronic gadget in a jar, it flickers like a firefly.

Caution: Always check your batteries to make sure they are the correct voltage. If too much electricity goes through the circuit, it can break components. When working with electrical components, always check the packaging for warnings.

THE STEPS

1. Place your NE555 timer chip between E13, E14, E15, E16, F13, F14, F15, and F16. Make sure the top legs of the chip are plugged into E13 and F13. There is a small half circle at the top of the chip.

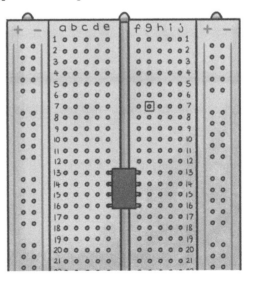

CONTINUED

2. Place one jumper wire between D14 and G15.

3. Place another jumper wire between G13 and D16.

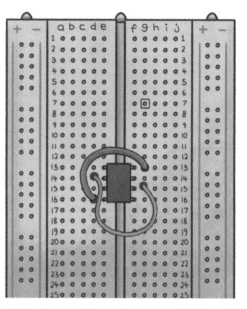

4. Place the 1K-ohm resistor between J13 and J14.

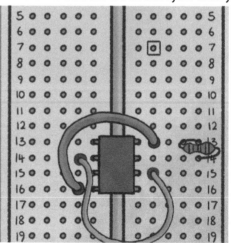

5. Place one 10K-ohm resistor between H14 and H15.

6. Place the remaining 10K-ohm resistor between I14 and I15.

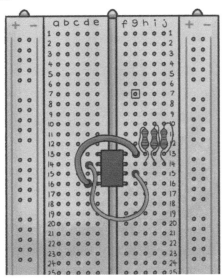

7. Place the remaining jumper wire between A13 and the left negative (−) channel on the left-hand side.

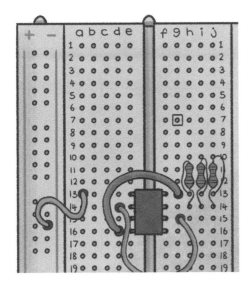

CONTINUED

8. Plug the positive (+) lead of your LED into B16 and the negative (−) lead into B15.

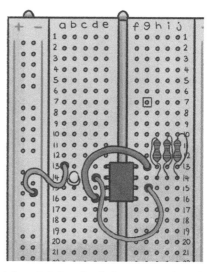

9. Plug the positive (+) lead of the capacitor into B14 and the negative (−) lead into B13.

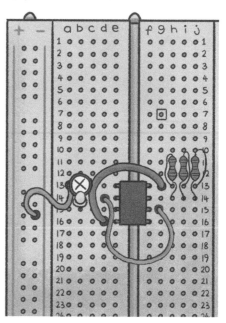

10. Put the battery in the battery holder. Plug the red wire of the battery holder into A16 and the black wire into the negative (–) channel on the left-hand side.

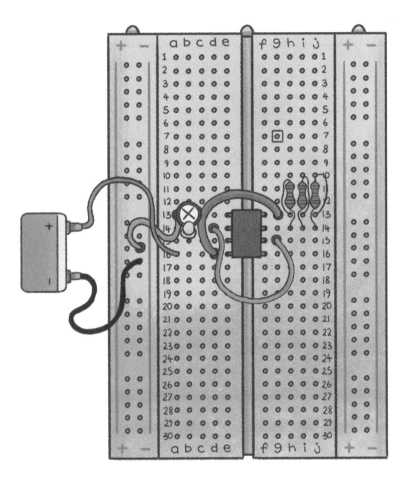

11. It's time to turn your circuit into a firefly. Draw a firefly on piece of paper and cut it out. Tape the paper over the top of the LED. Then gently put your breadboard into the jar. Be careful not to dislodge any of the components. You might need an adult to help you.

CONTINUED

The Hows and Whys: The capacitor changes the flow of electricity through your circuit. When the electricity flowing through your circuit changes, the light goes on and off. You could turn a switch on and off to make the same effect, but the capacitor does the work for you. It also keeps the blinking in a regular pattern.

STEAM CONNECTION: Your circuit is the main part of this art project. Many artists use science in their work. One of the first artists to use lights in sculpture was Keith Sonnier. He used neon light tubes and black paint to create contrasts between light and dark. In this art project, you created periods of light and dark as well.

Now Try This: Try using a microprocessor to make your circuit play music. What other art projects could you make using light and sound? What kind of music would you play in your projects?

MORSE CODE TELEGRAPH

Total time: 20 MINUTES

MATERIALS

- Breadboard
- 1 (4-pin) breadboard push button
- 2 jumper wires
- 1 LED (any color)
- 1 (5-volt) active buzzer
- 1 (9-volt) battery
- 1 (9-volt) battery holder with wire leads attached

Morse code is a method people can use to send information. A long time ago, folks would use a machine called a *telegraph* to send messages in Morse code to other people over long distances. How did it work? This project will show you how.

Caution: Always check your batteries to make sure they are the correct voltage. If too much electricity goes through the circuit, it can break components. When working with electrical components, always check the packaging for warnings.

THE STEPS

1. Place the breadboard push button between E63, E61, F63, and F61. This bridges the middle of your board.

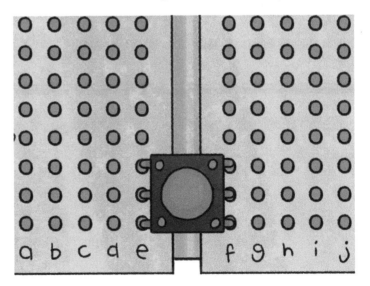

CONTINUED

2. Place one jumper wire between G61 and F20.

3. Place the remaining jumper wire between G20 and G10.

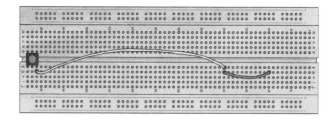

4. Plug the negative (–) lead of the LED into J10 and the positive (+) lead into the positive (+) channel on the right-hand side.

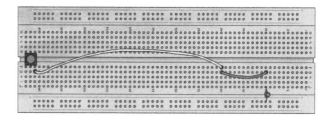

5. Plug the negative (–) lead of the buzzer into J61 and the positive (+) lead into the positive (+) channel on the right-hand side.

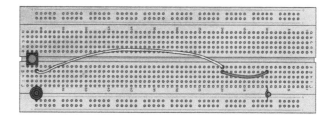

6. Put your battery in the battery holder. Plug the red wire of the battery holder into the right positive (+) channel and the black wire into D63.

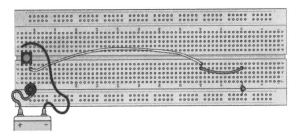

The Hows and Whys: The buzzer and the LED are wired in a series circuit. That means that the buzzer sounds before the LED lights. But because electricity moves so quickly, you probably can't see that the LED lights up after the buzzer sounds.

STEAM CONNECTION: Many years ago, before telephones and computers, the only way to send a message over a distance was to write a letter and mail it. This meant it could take anywhere from days or weeks to months for the message to be delivered. When the telegraph was invented, it was one of the first electric communication devices. People used it to send messages along wires through a series of taps and clicks called Morse code. This technology breakthrough meant that important messages could be delivered over long distances much faster.

CONTINUED

Now Try This: Send a secret message to a friend using your breadboard telegraph! Following the Morse code chart on the facing page, push the button on your telegraph to tap dots and dashes—use short pushes for dots and long pushes for dashes. Your friend should write down each sequence of dots and dashes they hear, then use the Morse code chart to decode the message.

HOW TO USE MORSE CODE

Use the chart below to send secret messages with your new device!

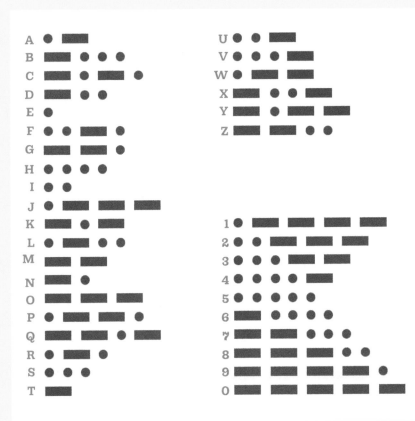

RED LIGHT, GREEN LIGHT

Total time: 30 MINUTES

MATERIALS

- Breadboard
- 2 jumper wires
- 2 (4-pin) breadboard push buttons
- 2 (470K-ohm) resistors
- 1 green LED
- 1 red LED
- 1 (9-volt) battery
- 1 (9-volt) battery holder with wire leads attached

Have you ever played Red Light, Green Light? In this game, players have to stop when someone says "red light" and can only move again when that person says "green light." But what if we wanted to play with friends who are deaf or hard of hearing? Or what if we wanted to play a sneaky spy version by making it a silent game? In this project, you're going to use your breadboard to update this game with technology!

 Caution: Always check your batteries to make sure they are the correct voltage. If too much electricity goes through the circuit, it can break components. When working with electrical components, always check the packaging for warnings.

THE STEPS

1. Place one jumper wire between G6 and the negative (–) channel on the right-hand side.

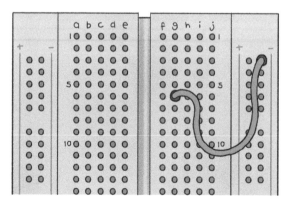

2. Place one breadboard push button between E6, F6, E8, and F8.

3. Place one resistor between G8 and G15.

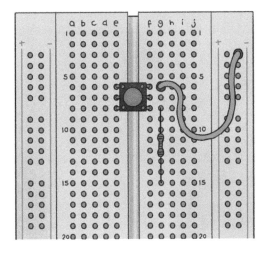

4. Plug the negative (−) lead of your green LED into J15 and the positive (+) lead into the positive (+) channel on the right-hand side.

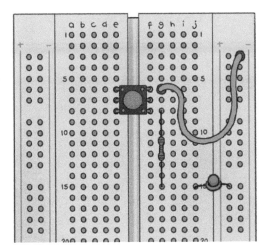

CONTINUED

5. Place the remaining jumper wire between G33 and the negative (−) channel on the right-hand side.

6. Place the remaining breadboard push button between E33, F33, E35, and F35.

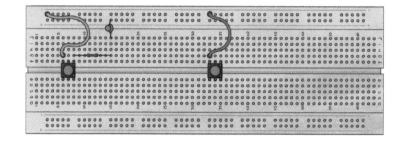

7. Place the remaining resistor between G35 and G41.

8. Plug the negative (−) lead of your red LED into J41 and the positive (+) lead into the positive (+) channel on the right-hand side.

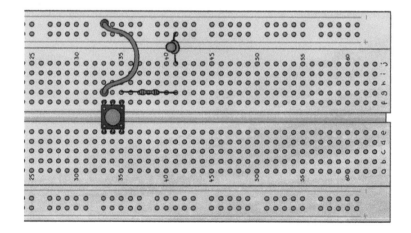

9. Put your battery in the battery holder. Plug the red wire from the battery holder into the positive (+) channel on the right-hand side and the black wire into the negative (−) channel on the same side. When you press the buttons, your LEDs light up.

The Hows and Whys: You made two simple circuits, each with a switch. This lets you do something a little different: your LEDs can be lit at the same time if you push both buttons. That means, though the circuits are separate, the electricity is running through your breadboard in parallel. You can light up one light, the other light, or both!

STEAM CONNECTION: By building this electronic device, you were able to modify an old game. Engineering different projects can help us make updates and see things in new ways. Engineers are constantly looking for ways to improve technology.

Now Try This: If you added a third circuit using a yellow LED, you could make your own push-button traffic light. Instead of making a game controller, you could make a timer. If you added the NE555 timer chip and a capacitor, you could make the lights flash at specific times.

ELECTRONIC DANCER

Total time: 30 TO 45 MINUTES

MATERIALS

- 1 sheet of cardstock
- 1 set of colored markers
- Ruler
- Scissors
- Clear tape
- 1 TT DC gearbox motor
- Breadboard
- 1 (4-pin) breadboard push button
- 2 LEDs (any color)
- 2 jumper wires
- 1 (9-volt) battery
- 1 (9-volt) battery holder with wires leads attached
- Connector wires

Get ready for a dance party! In this project, you'll make a dancer move and spin with a motor. You will also use LEDs so your dancer can put on a show!

Caution: Always check your batteries to make sure they are the correct voltage. If too much electricity goes through the circuit, it can break components. When working with electrical components, always check the packaging for warnings. Keep electronics turned off when not in use.

THE STEPS

1. Draw your dancer on the cardstock and color them. The dancer should be 2 to 3 inches in height.

2. Cut out your dancer, leaving ½ inch of extra cardstock at the bottom.

3. Fold the extra ½ inch of cardstock under your dancer. Tape this folded portion to the **axle** of the TT DC gearbox motor so the dancer stands upright. You want the dancer to go around in circles as the motor turns the axle.

4. Now start making your circuit. Place the push button between E25, E27, F25, and F27.

CONTINUED

5. Plug the short leg of your first LED into I20 and the long leg into the positive (+) channel on the right-hand side.

6. Plug the short leg of the remaining LED into I15 and the long leg into the positive (+) channel on the right-hand side.

7. Place one jumper wire between G25 and G20.

8. Place the remaining jumper wire between H25 and H15.

9. Plug the black wire of the motor into D25 and the red wire into the positive (+) channel on the right-hand side.

10. Put the battery in the battery holder. Plug the black wire of the battery holder into A27 and the red wire into the positive (+) channel on the right-hand side.

11. When you push the button, the LEDs light up and your dancer spins.

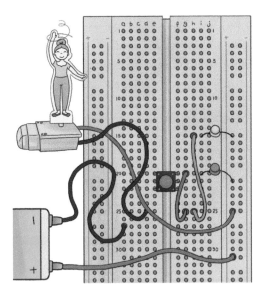

The Hows and Whys: When you run electricity through the circuit, the axle in the motor turns. In this circuit, the motor is our actuator. It works to make your dancer twirl.

CONTINUED

STEAM CONNECTION: This project shows how you can add art to almost anything in science or engineering. You created a picture that moved using a motor. Can you tell a story with this moving picture?

Now Try This: You can add more dancers to this project with additional motors. You could attach a fork to the axle to mix eggs in a bowl. What else could you attach to the axle on the motor? Think of ways this could help your everyday life.

BREADBOARD CAR

Total time: 30 MINUTES

MATERIALS

- 2 plastic wheels (that attach to the TT DC gearbox motor)
- 2 TT DC gearbox motors
- Adhesive-backed breadboard
- 1 (1-inch) swivel caster wheel
- 1 (9-volt) battery
- 1 (9-volt) battery holder with wire leads attached

Start your engines! In this project, you will build a car that really moves on wheels.

! **Caution:** Always check your batteries to make sure they are the correct voltage. If too much electricity goes through the circuit, it can break components. When working with electrical components, always check the packaging for warnings.

THE STEPS

1. Slide one plastic wheel onto one axle of a TT DC gearbox motor. Then slide the remaining plastic wheel onto one axle of the remaining motor.

2. Peel off the backing on the underside of the breadboard to expose the adhesive.

3. Stick your motors to the underside of the breadboard. The motors need to face opposite directions. This will allow your wheels to turn in the same direction.

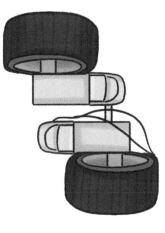

CONTINUED

4. Stick your caster wheel to the underside of the breadboard as shown.

5. Connect the red wires from each motor to the positive (+) channel on the right-hand side.

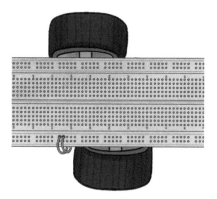

6. Plug the black wire from one motor into H30. Plug the black wire from the second motor into I30.

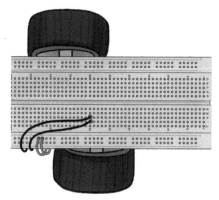

7. Put the battery in the battery holder. Plug the red wire from the battery holder into the positive (+) channel on the right-hand side. Plug the black wire into G30. Once the battery is connected to the circuit, each motor will spin its wheel. Set it down and watch it go!

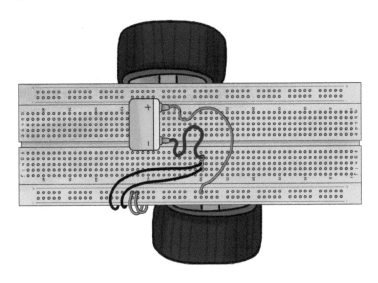

The Hows and Whys: The battery acts as your power source to turn the axles of your motors. This is the same way a real car operates. In this project, you built two circuits with motors in parallel. Did you notice that one motor faces the back of the car and the other motor faces the front? That's because the wheels are actually on opposite sides of your motors. You need to change the way the motors face to make the wheels go the same direction. You could also swap the **polarity** of the wires. To do this, connect your battery wires to the opposite motor wires. The wheels will spin in the opposite direction.

CONTINUED

STEAM CONNECTION: Cars need a lot of engineering and technology to run smoothly. But the way a car looks is also important to carmakers. With some cardboard, markers, and scissors, you can add an artistic design to the car you made in this project.

Now Try This: See if you can extend this project by building a wind-powered vehicle. Instead of putting wheels on your motors, could you attach fans to propel the car forward? How else could you convert this car?

BUBBLE BLOWER

Total time: 20 MINUTES

MATERIALS

- 1 low-voltage, low-current DC motor
- 1 propeller fan (that fits on the low-voltage, low-current DC motor)
- Breadboard
- 1 (4-pin) breadboard push button
- 1 jumper wire
- 1 (9-volt) battery
- 1 (9-volt) battery holder with wire leads attached
- 1 plastic bag
- 1 bottle of bubble solution
- 1 bubble wand

You don't need to huff and puff to blow bubbles into the air. This cool device will do all the work for you. Using a motor and a fan, you're going to make an automatic bubble blower.

Caution: Do NOT get your circuit wet! Adult supervision is required for this project. Always check your batteries to make sure they are the correct voltage. If too much electricity goes through the circuit, it can break components. When working with electrical components, always check the packaging for warnings.

THE STEPS

1. Attach the fan to the motor.

2. Place the push button between E2, E4, F2, and F4.

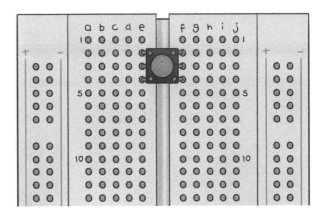

CONTINUED

3. Plug the red wire of the motor into the right-hand positive (+) channel and the black wire into H2.

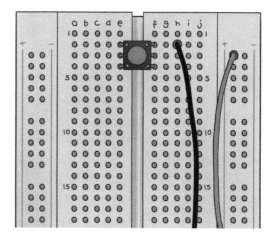

4. Place the jumper wire between D4 and D20.

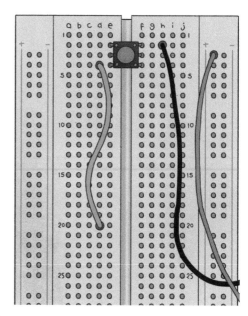

5. Put the battery in the battery holder. Plug the red wire of the battery holder into the positive (+) channel on the right-hand side and the black wire into B20.

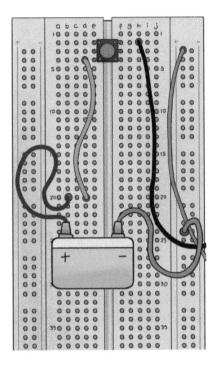

6. Put your breadboard circuit into the plastic bag to make sure the breadboard stays dry. (You can also use a dishcloth or rag.) Make sure the fan is outside of the bag.

7. Position the fan so it can spin when you push the button. Then dip the bubble wand into the bubble solution. Hold the wand in front of the fan. Now push the button.

CONTINUED

The Hows and Whys: When you push the button, it completes the circuit. This makes the actuator—the fan—do its work. You have used electricity to turn a motor and make wind!

STEAM CONNECTION: Have you ever seen a wind turbine? It looks like a giant fan. You might think it works like the fan in this project, but it's actually the opposite: electricity makes your fan spin, but a turbine uses the wind outside to turn a motor and generate electricity. Scientists and engineers have found different ways to make electricity.

Now Try This: How would you extend this project to design a helicopter? Try adding another motor and fan. You'll need to place a DC motor at either side of your breadboard so that they face upward. Make the helicopter as light as you can so it can fly!

ALARM CLOCK

MATERIALS

- Breadboard
- 1 (5-volt) active buzzer
- 1 (5-millimeter) photoresistor
- 1 BC547 transistor
- 1 (1K-ohm) resistor
- 3 jumper wires
- 1 (9-volt) battery holder
- 1 (9-volt) battery holder with wire leads attached

Make your own alarm clock that buzzes when the sun rises. You won't sleep in with the help of this electronic device.

Caution: Always check your batteries to make sure they are the correct voltage. If too much electricity goes through the circuit, it can break components. When working with electrical components, always check the packaging for warnings.

THE STEPS

1. Plug the positive (+) lead of the buzzer into H1 and the negative (−) lead into H4.

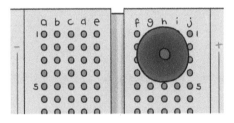

2. Place the photoresistor between F1 and F11.

CONTINUED

3. Place the transistor between G9, G11, and G13. The flat side of your transistor should face the left-hand side of the breadboard.

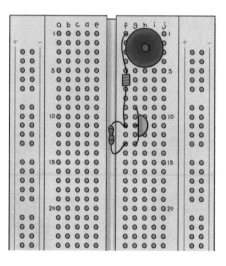

4. Place the resistor between F11 and F13. You will notice that the photoresistor also has a lead in F11.

5. Place one jumper wire between J1 and the positive (+) channel of the right-hand side.

6. Place a second jumper wire between J4 and H9.

7. Place the remaining jumper wire between H13 and the negative (–) channel on the right-hand side.

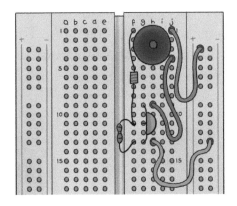

8. Put the battery in the battery holder. Plug the red wire from the battery holder into the positive (+) channel on the right-hand side and the black wire into the negative (–) channel on the right-hand side. Test your alarm clock by turning the lights in the room on and off.

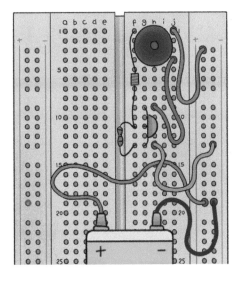

CONTINUED

The Hows and Whys: Photoresistors change their resistance depending on how much light is present. When light touches the photoresistor, tiny particles in the light called **photons** make the electrons move. The electrons jump between the conductive wires in the photoresistor. With these extra electrons moving, the resistance of the photoresistor decreases and more electricity can move through the circuit. This is how your buzzer is powered when the light shines on the photoresistor.

STEAM CONNECTION: **Levi Hutchins built the first modern alarm clock in 1787 by using an existing mechanical clock. He modified it to make a bell ring when the gears in the clock turned to 4:00 a.m. Inventors modify things in order to solve problems.**

Now Try This: This alarm clock is designed to buzz when light hits the photoresistor. Can you change this device into a bedtime alarm that buzzes when it gets dark? (Hint: Try designing a circuit where the actuator works when the resistance is lower.)

ELECTRIC SKILL GAME

Total time: 1 HOUR

MATERIALS

- Breadboard
- 1 red LED
- 3 jumper wires
- 1 (5-volt) active buzzer
- 1 (9-volt) battery
- 1 (9-volt) battery holder with wire leads attached
- 1 (12-inch by 12-inch) piece of cardboard
- Scissors
- Copper tape
- Clear tape
- Metal tweezers

In this project, build an electronic game that you can play with friends. The goal is to pick up an object with a pair of tweezers without touching the game board. If you touch the board, the board will flash and buzz. Game on!

Caution: Ask an adult if you need help cutting the cardboard. The copper tape has sharp edges that can cut you, so be careful when working with it. Always check your batteries to make sure they are the correct voltage. If too much electricity goes through the circuit, it can break components. When working with electrical components, always check the packaging for warnings.

THE STEPS

1. Plug the negative (−) lead of the LED into J4 and the positive (+) lead into the positive (+) channel on the right-hand side.

CONTINUED

2. Place one jumper wire between G4 and G12.

3. Place a second jumper wire between F12 and F33.

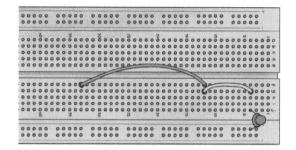

4. Plug the negative (+) lead of the buzzer into J33 and the positive (+) lead into the positive (+) channel on the right-hand side.

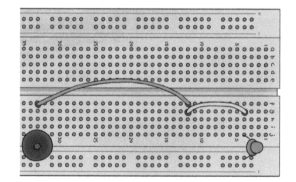

5. Put the battery in the battery holder. Now test your circuit by plugging the black wire from the battery holder into I33 and the red wire into the positive (+) channel on the right-hand side. If the circuit is working, the buzzer will sound and the LED will light up.

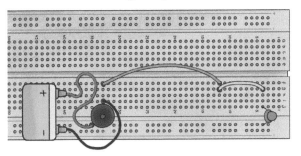

6. Now start making your game board. Cut a 1-inch square out of the middle of the piece of cardboard.

7. Apply copper tape around the edges of the square hole. The circuit will work much better if you use only one piece of copper tape all the way around the hole.

8. Use clear tape to attach one end of the remaining jumper wire to the copper tape. Plug the other end of the wire into I33.

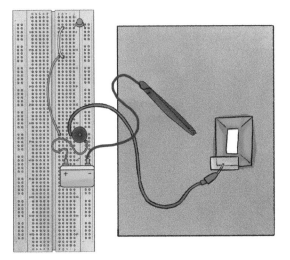

CONTINUED

9. Wrap the black wire of the battery holder around the head of the tweezers. Use clear tape to attach the wire to the tweezers.

10. Time to play! Place a small object in the square hole of your game board; it should be smaller than 1 inch by 1 inch so it will fit in the hole. You can use a building block, a toy figurine, or a crumpled ball of paper. Now use the tweezers to see if you can lift the object out of the hole without setting off the buzzer and LED.

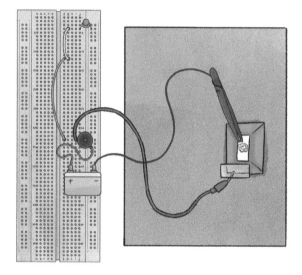

The Hows and Whys: You built a series circuit. If the metal tweezers touch the copper tape, it completes the circuit and activates the buzzer and LED. You can make as many game pieces and connections as you want for this game.

STEAM CONNECTION: Games are a great way to learn different problem-solving skills. To create board games, puzzles, and video games, engineers and designers have to use all the different parts of STEAM together.

Now Try This: Can you make an electronic version of tic-tac-toe? Try to design a circuit with LEDs that light when players use a square. What other games can you build with your breadboard?

HEAT DETECTOR

MATERIALS

- Breadboard
- 1 2N2222 transistor
- 1 (330K-ohm) resistor
- 1 (4.7K-ohm) resistor
- 1 (1K-ohm) thermistor
- 1 (5-volt) active buzzer
- 1 (9-volt) battery
- 1 (9-volt) battery holder with wire leads attached

Is it getting hot in here? Build an electronic detector to find out! Using your breadboard, you can use a **thermistor** to make a heat alarm.

> **!** **Caution:** Adult supervision is required for this project. You must ask an adult to provide a match or lighter. Always have an adult supervise or help when you work with an open flame.

THE STEPS

1. Place the transistor between J25, J27, and J29. The curved side of the transistor should face the right-hand side of the breadboard.

2. Place the 330K-ohm resistor between I25 and H23.

3. Place the 4.7K-ohm resistor between G23 and I27.

CONTINUED

4. Place the thermistor between F23 and F32.

5. Plug the positive (+) lead of the buzzer into I32 and the negative (−) lead into I29.

6. Put the battery in the battery holder. Plug the red wire of the battery holder into F32 and the black wire into H25.

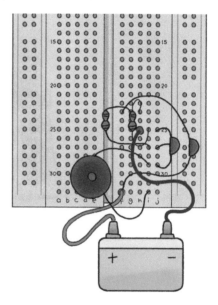

7. Now test your circuit. Ask an adult to hold a lit match or lighter near your thermistor for a few seconds. The buzzer will start beeping. To stop the beeping, disconnect the battery wires.

The Hows and Whys: Your project works just like a smoke detector. However, instead of sensing smoke, your sensor detects the heat from a fire. Inside a smoke detector, there is a small amount of material that reacts with smoke. This material lies between two conductive plates. When smoke reaches this material, it causes a break in the flow of electricity, which sets off an alarm.

STEAM CONNECTION: Sensors are used in many devices to keep us safe. At a crosswalk, you hear chirping when the light tells you to walk. The chirping sound helps people who are blind or visually impaired know when it's safe to cross the street. Circuits can be designed to help people live more safely.

Now Try This: How would you use a different sensor in this project? Remember the circuits you made that detected sound or movement. See if you can switch out the parts on the breadboard to make a different effect.

FLASHING METRONOME

Total time: 40 MINUTES

MATERIALS

- Breadboard
- 1 NE555 timer chip
- 2 jumper wires
- 1 (1K-ohm) resistor
- 2 (10K-ohm) resistors
- 2 LEDs (any color)
- 1 (1-µF) capacitor
- 1 (10-µF) capacitor
- 1 (100-µF) capacitor
- 1 (9-volt) battery
- 1 (9-volt) battery holder with wire leads attached

A metronome is a tool that musicians use to keep the beat of music they are playing. The metronome ticks or beeps at a specific pace, or tempo. You can build a metronome that makes two lights flash in tempo.

Caution: Always check your batteries to make sure they are the correct voltage. If too much electricity goes through the circuit, it can break components. When working with electrical components, always check the packaging for warnings. As always, disconnect the power source when you are not using your circuit.

THE STEPS

1. Place the timer chip between E13, E14, E15, E16, F13, F14, F15, and F16. Make sure the top legs of the chip are plugged into E13 and F13. There is a small half circle at the top of the chip.

2. Place one jumper wire between D14 and G15.

3. Place the remaining jumper wire between G13 and D16.

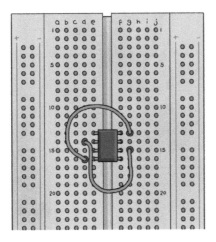

4. Place the 1K-ohm resistor between D15 and D16.

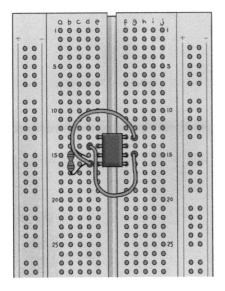

5. Place one 10K-ohm resistor between A14 and A15.

CONTINUED

6. Place the remaining 10K-ohm resistor between B14 and B15.

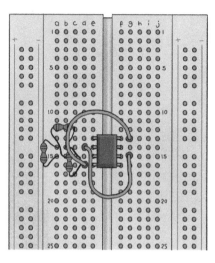

7. Plug the positive (+) lead of one LED into J13 and the negative (−) lead into J14.

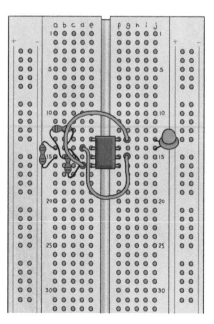

8. Plug the positive (+) lead of the remaining LED into I14 and the negative (−) lead into H15.

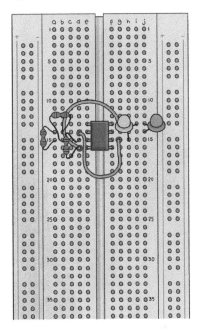

9. Plug the long leg of the 1-µF capacitor into J15 and the short leg into I16.

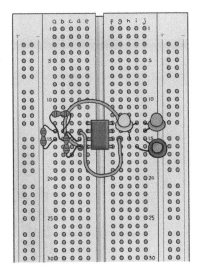

CONTINUED

10. Put the battery in the battery holder. Plug the red wire of the battery holder into I13 and the black wire into G16. The LED will flash.

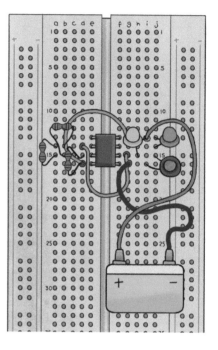

11. If you change the voltage of the capacitor, the LED flashes at a different speed. Unplug the 1-µF capacitor and replace it with the 10-µF capacitor.

12. Next, unplug the 10-µF capacitor and replace it with the 100-µF capacitor. The LED will blink at a different speed.

The Hows and Whys: The capacitor blocks the current of electricity and creates a pulsing current. This pulsing electricity is what makes the LED flash at a regular interval. When you change the voltage of the capacitor, the LED flashes at a different speed.

Now Try This: You could make your metronome with a buzzer by changing the capacitors and actuators. You can use the timer chip to create sound at regular intervals if you change the resistance and the actuator. How else can you use a timer?

Chapter 3

PUTTING IT ALL TOGETHER

Congratulations! You finished the book! By doing these projects, you didn't just make electronics—you analyzed problems, came up with solutions, and figured out how to improve your creations. Do you know what that means? You are an electrical engineer!

Now you understand how circuits work. So, what can you do with all this knowledge? Think of different electronic devices you could build. The projects in this book are just a starting point. Keep asking questions and solving problems.

The more you invent and create, the more opportunities you will uncover. There are so many careers that involve electronics, from car mechanic to computer programmer to fashion designer. You can explore different paths as your interests grow, too. For example, Rune Elmqvist invented the pacemaker, a small electronic device that sends electric pulses to the heart to keep it on a regular beat. His invention has saved thousands of people's lives. Although his career started in medicine as a doctor, he became an inventor when he saw how he could help people by using electronics. As the world continues to change, you can dream up new ways to improve the future.

GLOSSARY

ACTUATOR: Part of a circuit or machine that makes something move. Some examples of actuators are motors, valves, and buzzers.

ANODE: The positively charged end of a device that lets electrons into the circuit.

ATOM: The smallest unit of matter.

BREADBOARD: A board that is used for prototyping electronic or circuit builds.

CAPACITOR: Something that holds or stores energy within an electric field or circuit. A capacitor is different from a battery because it stores potential energy as electric energy; a battery stores potential energy in chemical form.

CATHODE: The negatively charged end of a device.

CHARGE: The physical property of matter that causes it to respond to an electric field. Electric charges can be positive or negative. When atoms give off or receive extra electrons, they become charged. This means that they will gravitate toward or away from atoms with different or similar charges.

CIRCUIT: A route through which electricity moves.

COMPONENT: Part of a circuit.

CONDUCTIVE: Something that helps heat or electricity move between objects.

CURRENT: The flow of electrons through a conductor. In a circuit, the current can be measured in amperes (usually shortened to "amps").

ELECTRICITY: A type of energy made up of charged particles, like electrons, that can be delivered through a current, or flow of charge.

ELECTROLYTE: A liquid containing ions, which can conduct electricity.

ELECTRON: Part of an atom that is negatively charged.

ENERGY: The ability to do work or move matter. Energy comes in many forms, such as electric energy, solar energy, and mechanical energy.

INSULATOR: Something that resists the flow of electrons through it, thus preventing the flow of electricity. Insulators are poor conductors.

ION: An atom that has an electric charge.

LED: An acronym for light-emitting diode. An LED is a conductor that glows when an electric current flows through it.

MICROPROCESSOR: A small programmable object that works like a computer to follow the directions programmed into it. Microprocessors can process data, read binary, receive input, and generate output instructions.

PARALLEL CIRCUIT: A type of circuit where components are connected in parallel. This allows the electric current to flow through components simultaneously. The voltage across the parallel ends of the circuit is the same even if the current varies.

PHOTORESISTOR: An electric component whose resistance varies depending on the amount of light energy focused on it. As the photoresistor receives more light, it lowers its resistance.

POWER SOURCE: The place in a circuit in which power is stored. A battery is a common power source.

RESISTANCE: The measurement of how difficult it is for electricity to flow through something. Resistance is measured in ohms.

RESISTOR: A component that increases the resistance or lessens the flow of electricity within a circuit.

SENSOR: A circuit component that is used to detect something and activate a response to that input.

SERIES CIRCUIT: A type of circuit that is designed to have the electric current flow through each component before proceeding to the next component. This means the voltage drops after each component.

SWITCH: A controllable break in the conductive path of a circuit. When the switch is closed, electricity flows through the circuit. When the switch is open, electricity cannot flow through the circuit.

THERMISTOR: A type of resistor whose resistance is dependent on the temperature. When the temperature increases, the resistance increases. When the temperature decreases, the resistance decreases.

TRANSISTOR: An electric component that acts as a fast switch in a circuit and can also amplify, or increase, the current in a circuit.

VOLTAGE: The pressure at which electrons are pushed from a power source. This is the way we measure the flow of electrons in a circuit. It is measured in volts.

RESOURCES

For more information on paper circuits:
Chibitronics.com/education/or technolojie.com/sketching-in-circuits

For more sewable circuit project ideas and directions:
ChaosLearningLab.Weebly.com
L. Buechley, K. Qiu, and Sonja de Boer, *Sew Electric: A Collection of DIY Projects That Combine Fabric, Electronics, and Programming* (Cambridge, MA: HLT Press, 2013).

For more information on robotics:
Instructables.com/simple-robotics-breadboard

INDEX

ACKNOWLEDGMENTS

My thanks to the team at Callisto, who smoothly stewarded this project and deserve so much credit. Special thanks to my editor, Eliza Kirby. This book is infinitely richer because of your feedback.

As an educator, I cannot ignore the powerful impact my own teachers had on me. Mrs. Santarsiero, you gave me a love of learning and kickball that survives to this day. Mr. Rue, you made me fall in love with science in every form. And Mr. C., my high school physics teacher who told me "girls don't do physics"—I guess some of us do.

In my 20 years in education, I have been truly blessed to have students who challenge and inspire me every year. Many of the lessons reflected in this book come from learning from all of them. Drs. Yasmin Kafai and Deborah Fields introduced me to the joys and challenges of electronic textiles. I also want to acknowledge the wisdom and expertise of my student and colleague Douglas Ball, the best physics teacher I know!

Professionally, I could not have been more blessed than to start my academic career at Utah State University. Dr. Beth Foley made so much possible for me, and I am forever in her debt. My colleagues Kimberly Lott and Max Longhurst are the best team I could have hoped to join. Andrea Hawkman, Beth MacDonald, and Mario Suarez: I learn so much from you every day. Kristin Searle, the entirety of this book is not enough space to explicate your impact or express my gratitude for you. My work and my person are better for your partnership.

Lastly, I want to acknowledge the impact of my family. A person would be lucky to be born into a loving family, which I was. Amazingly, I was blessed to marry into one as well. Thank you Steve and Diane, for your support no matter what deadlines popped up mid-family visit. To my nieces and nephews, Snake, Quinn, Hank, and Jack, thank you for testing the projects in this book and asking amazing questions. Grandma and Grandpa, your support and love let me dream impossible things. Peter, this is all your fault, because you told me to write a book; thank you. Dad, I would not feel your absence so keenly had your presence not been so profound. Mom, you are the first woman in STEM I knew and my best example of how to do it. Atticus, Jacob, Hank, and Phin, thank you for your wisdom, your humor, and the sharp focus you bring to my life. Being your mom is my favorite job. Finally, David, everything starts and ends with you. You are my first editor, my barista, and my best friend all wrapped up in one. Thank you for the support, the laughter, and the copious amounts of coffee. Now please go finish your book.

ABOUT THE AUTHOR

 **Dr. Colby Tofel-Grehl** (she/her) is an associate professor of teacher education at Utah State University and director of the Chaos Learning Lab. Her research focuses on bringing new technology into classrooms and igniting student interest in STEAM. As a former elementary school teacher, Dr. Tofel-Grehl understands the need for children to learn from interest-driven learning experiences that are scaffolded to support them along the way. In 2020, she was honored with the Association for Science Teacher Education Teacher of the Year Award.